JANICE VANCLEAVE'S
FIRST-PLACE SCIENCE FAIR PR

D0124259

STEP-BY-STE
SCIENCE EXPERIMENTS IN

CHEMISTRY

rosen publishing's
rosen central®

NEW YORK

This edition first published in 2013 by:

The Rosen Publishing Group, Inc.
29 East 21st Street
New York, NY 10010

Library of Congress Cataloging-in-Publication Data

VanCleave, Janice Pratt.
Step-by-step science experiments in chemistry/Janice VanCleave.
    p. cm.—(Janice Vancleave's first-place science fair projects)
Includes bibliographical references and index.
ISBN 978-1-4488-6981-7 (lib. bdg.)—ISBN 978-1-4488-8465-0 (pbk.)—
ISBN 978-1-4488-8466-7 (6-pack)
1. Chemistry—Experiments—Juvenile literature. I. Title.
QD38.V374 2013
540.78—dc23

2012007947

Manufactured in the United States of America

CPSIA Compliance Information: Batch #S12YA: For further information, contact Rosen Publishing, New York, New York, at 1-800-237-9932.

This edition published by arrangement with and permission of John Wiley & Sons, Inc., Hoboken, New Jersey.

Originally published as *Chemistry for Every Kid.* Copyright © 1989 by John Wiley & Sons, Inc.

CONTENTS

INTRODUCTION

Chemistry is the study of the way materials are put together and their behavior under different conditions. This science, more than any other, involves all of one's senses: seeing, hearing, tasting, feeling, and smelling. It is a springboard into other scientific fields. A foundation in basic chemistry facts can assist one in the study of other scientific curricula. One cannot explain the physics concept of magnetism or electricity without understanding the chemistry of atoms. The biological study of photosynthesis has more meaning with the knowledge of the basic chemical reactions involved. Many examples for each scientific field can be given that stress the usefulness of chemistry but, besides this application, chemistry concepts can be used to explain many events we observe in daily life.

The history of chemistry essentially started over three thousand years ago, when ancient Babylonians began to record the known metals. In 430 BCE, Democritis proclaimed that all matter was composed of atoms. Around 300 BCE, Aristotle proposed the existence of only four elements: fire, air, water, and earth.

But it was the alchemists who can truly take credit for the rise of experimentation with the elements. Alchemists sought in vain to transform everything imaginable into gold. All of their efforts to produce gold failed. These so-called "mad scientists" are the forefathers of experimentation. They spent time studying the problem, designed innumerable experiments and, unlike other scientists of their day, they actually experimented. Special equipment was not available for them to order through science catalogs. They designed and made all of the needed flasks and beakers. Some of these designs, in modified form, are still used today in our modern chemistry laboratories.

These chemists of the past were the first to use what is now described as the scientific method, a logical approach to the solution of a problem through experimentation. This process underlies all of the experiments in this book. The alchemists may have failed to solve their problem of changing a base material into gold, but they set the stage for future scientific discoveries. Their dream was partially fulfilled after two thousand years when in 1941, Kenneth T. Bainbridge, an American physicist, changed mercury into gold. The gold produced did not fill a pot, but rather was microscopic in size and was more expensive to produce than the gold was worth.

Even today, just the mention of the word "chemistry" too often conjures up the image of a mad scientist hovering over strange, bubbling flasks. Unfortunately, explosions, danger, and flesh-eating acids are associated with chemistry, so many students might be understandably wary about conducting experiments of their own. "Are there any chemicals in there?" is a frequently asked question.

This book will relieve the fears of performing chemistry experiments by acquainting the reader with "chemicals."

As knowledge about chemistry is gained by performing these fun and safe experiments, the fear of experimenting will be replaced with a desire to know more about the subject.

All of the experiments in this book are basic enough for a person not familiar with scientific terms to understand. The results are dramatic but expected, thus no frightening experiences. Mysterious experiments will be performed—clear liquids change into a green blob, pennies acquire green coats, colors disappear, and many others. Not all of the experiments are magical in nature, but all stir the interest of young and old alike with the wonders and the fun of chemistry. It is hoped that these pleasing chemistry experiences will be used to encourage new chemistry students to seek further knowledge not only in the chemistry field, but also in science in general.

Even with our vast knowledge of chemistry, there is still so very much to be learned and discovered. Few clues are available as to how a simple plant uses water from the soil, carbon dioxide from the air, and light energy from the sun to produce stored food, a process called photosynthesis. There are many opportunities in the field of chemistry for a person with an inquisitive mind and a spirit of adventure. Much is yet to be learned, but great fun and excitement is in store for the beginning scientist in discovering the chemistry secrets that have already been unlocked.

This book will bring the image of chemistry out of the professional chemistry laboratory and into daily-life experiences. It is designed to present technical chemistry theories in such a way that a person with little or no science training can understand. The experiments are selected based on their ability to be explained basically and on their lack of complexity. A big factor in choosing them was their dramatic appeal. One of the main objectives of the book is to present the fun of chemistry.

The reader will be rewarded with successful experiments if he or she reads an experiment carefully, follows each step in order, and does not substitute equipment. It is suggested that the experiments within a group be performed in order. There is some buildup of information from the first to the last, but any terms defined in a previous experiment can be found in the glossary.

When beginning each experiment, you will see several individual sections, as detailed below.

- Purpose: This states the basic goals for the experiment.
- Materials: A list of necessary supplies.
- Procedure: Step-by-step instructions on how to perform the experiment.
- Results: An explanation exactly stating what is expected to happen. This is an immediate learning tool. If the expected results are achieved, the experimenter has an immediate positive reinforcement. A "foul-up" is also quickly recognized, and the need to start over or make corrections is readily apparent.
- Why?: An explanation of why the results were achieved is described in understandable terms. This means it is understandable to the reader who may not be familiar with scientific terms.

Take your time to read over the instructions carefully before you begin. And most importantly, have fun!

SUPER CHAIN

PURPOSE: To observe physical properties and their changes.

FACTS: Physical properties are descriptions about a substance that can be made by seeing, hearing, tasting, feeling, or smelling the material.

MATERIALS:
- 3×5-inch (7.62 x 12.7 cm) index card
- scissors

PROCEDURE:

1. Observe the following physical properties of the index card: color, shape, size, and texture (how it feels).
2. Fold the index card in half along the long side.
3. Before starting the cuts, note the following things:

   A. All of the cuts are to be about one-quarter inch (6.5 mm) apart and end at least one-quarter inch (6.5 mm) from the edge.

   B. The cuts should alternate from the folded edge to the open edge.

4. Start at one end. Make the first cut across the fold stopping one-quarter inch (6.5 mm) from the open edge.

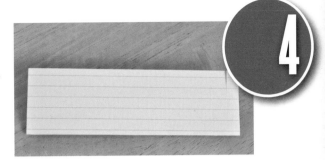

5. The second cut starts at the open edge and stops one-quarter inch (6.5 mm) from the folded edge.

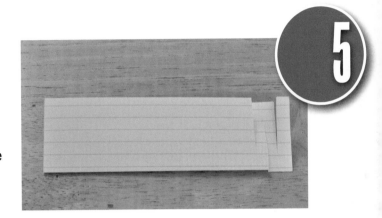

6. Alternate the cuts from the folded side to the open edge. Be careful to stop within one-quarter inch (6.5 mm) from each edge.

7. Slip the point of your scissors under the fold at point (A) and cut the fold until you reach point (B). Important: Do not cut the fold on the two end pieces.

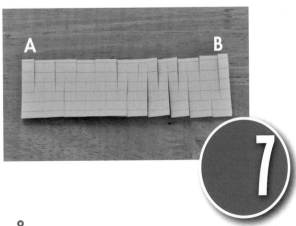

8. Carefully stretch the card open to form a large chain.

9. Observe the physical properties of the index card again: color, shape, size, and texture.

RESULTS The color and texture of the card have not changed, but the size and shape of the card have. It was a 3x5-inch (7.62 x 12.7 cm) rectangular, paper card, but after the cutting it resulted in a zigzag chainlike structure big enough to slip around a person's body.

WHY? The procedure for cutting produced the same effect as cutting thin strips from the card and connecting them. The zigzag structure allows the paper to stretch out into a large super chain.

HOW MUCH?

PURPOSE: To demonstrate that 1 + 1 does not always equal two.

MATERIALS:

- clear glass quart (.9 ml) jar
- 1 cup (200 g) of sugar
- measuring cup
- masking tape
- pencil or pen

PROCEDURE:

1. Place a strip of masking tape down the outside of the jar.

2. Pour 1 cup (240 ml) of water into the jar.

3. Mark the water level on the tape.

4. Add a second cup of water to the jar and again mark the water level on the tape.

5. Empty and dry the measuring jar.

6. Pour 1 cup (200 g) of sugar into the jar. Make sure that the top of the sugar is at the 1-cup mark on the tape.

7. Add 1 cup (240 ml) of water.

8. Stir.

9. Observe the level of the water.

RESULTS The liquid level is below the 2-cup mark on the tape.

WHY? Water and sugar are examples of matter and cannot occupy the same space at the same time. The cup of sugar is not solid throughout. There are spaces between the sugar grains. The water moves into these spaces, resulting in a volume that is less than 2 cups.

NO HEAT

PURPOSE: To make water appear to boil with only the touch from a finger.

MATERIALS:

- cotton handkerchief
- clear drinking glass
  (with straight, smooth sides)
- rubber band

PROCEDURE:

1. Wet the handkerchief with water. Squeeze out any excess water.

2. Fill the glass to the top with water.

3. Drape the wet cloth over the mouth of the glass.

4. Place the rubber band over the cloth in the middle of the glass to hold the cloth close to the glass.

5. Use your fingers to push the cloth down about 1 inch (2.54 cm) below the water level.

6. Pick the glass up, hold the bottom with one hand, and turn it upside down. Note: There will be some spillage, so do this over a sink.

7. Place the other hand under the hanging cloth and hold the glass. At this point one hand is holding the cloth next to the glass with the free end of the cloth draped over this hand

8. With the free hand push down on the bottom of the glass. Allow the glass to slowly slip down into the cloth.

RESULTS The water does not fall out of the glass, and it appears to start boiling.

WHY? Water does not flow out of the cloth because the tiny holes in the cloth are filled with water. Water molecules have a strong attraction for each other, which draws them close together. This causes the water to behave as if a thin skin were covering each hole in the cloth, preventing the water in the glass from falling out.

Pushing the glass down causes the cloth to be pulled out of the glass. This outward movement of the cloth creates a vacuum inside and the air outside is pushed through the cloth. Small bubbles of air form inside the water, giving an appearance of boiling water.

TUG OF WAR

PURPOSE: To demonstrate the difference in the pulling power of water and alcohol.

MATERIALS:

- 1-foot (30 cm) sheet of aluminum foil
- food coloring (red or blue)
- rubbing alcohol
- water
- eyedropper
- 2 cups

PROCEDURE:

1. Add enough food coloring to ½ cup (120 mL) of water to make a dark solution.

2. Fill a second cup one-quarter (60 ml) full with alcohol.

3

3. Smooth the sheet of aluminum foil on a table.

4. Pour a very thin layer of the colored water onto the foil. Note: The thinner the water, the better.

4

5. Use the eye-dropper to add a drop of alcohol to the center of the thin layer of col-ored water.

RESULTS The water rushes away from the alcohol, leaving a very thin layer of alcohol on the foil. The water is pulling, and this causes a pulsation around the edges of the alcohol.

WHY? The water molecules on the surface of the water are pulling equally in all directions before the alcohol is added. When the drop of alcohol touches the water, there is an immediate separation between the two liquids. Alcohol is pulling away from the water and the water is pulling away from the alcohol. The water molecules seem to be victorious, and the water spreads outward, taking some of the alcohol with it. This outward movement causes the alcohol to be spread into a thin layer over the foil. It also causes the water molecules to stack up and form a ridge around the alcohol layer. This ridge has a pulsating motion because the water and alcohol molecules continue to pull on each other. The pulling stops when the two liquids totally mix together.

ANTI-GRAVITY?

PURPOSE: A demonstration of overcoming the forces of gravity.

MATERIALS:

- 1 small baby food jar
- 1 straw
- red or blue food coloring
- clay, a piece the size of a marble

PROCEDURE:

1. Press the clay against the inside of the bottom of the jar.

2. Fill the jar one-half full with water.

3. Add three or four drops of food coloring to the water and stir.

4. Slowly lower the straw into the colored water.

5. Push the bottom end of the straw into the clay. The straw can now stand in a vertical position.

6. Quickly turn the jar upside down over a sink.

7. Turn the jar right side up and set it on a table.

8. Observe the liquid level inside the straw, if any.

RESULTS Colored water remains in the straw. The height of the water in the straw is the same as that of the water before it was poured out.

WHY? Water molecules are attracted to each other. At the surface of the water, the molecules tug on each other so much that a skin-like surface is produced. The air in the straw pushes up on the water when the jar is inverted and water molecules are pulling from side to side. These forces are greater than the downward force of gravity; thus the water remains in the straw.

MIND OF ITS OWN

PURPOSE: To observe the movement of paper circles that seem to have a mind of their own.

MATERIALS:

- piece of notebook paper
- paper hole punch
- eyedropper
- toothpick
- small glass with no more than a 2-inch (5 cm) diameter (candle holder or an egg holder will work)

PROCEDURE:

1. Use the hole punch to cut three or four circles from the paper.

2. Fill the glass about three-quarters full with water.

3. When the water is calm, place a paper circle on the surface in the center.

RESULTS After a few seconds, the paper moves to the side.

4. Add two more paper circles, and using the toothpick, move the circles to the center of the water.

RESULTS The paper continues to move toward the edge.

5. Remove the paper and fill the glass to overflowing with water. Use the eyedropper to add the extra drops needed to make the water bulge above the sides of the glass.

6. When the water is calm, place the paper circles in the center.

7. Use the toothpick to move the circles toward the edge carefully; then release them. Be sure that you do not force the water over the edge of the glass. Repeat.

RESULTS The paper continues to move toward the center of the water.

WHY? Surface water molecules pull on each other, but they are more attracted to the molecules in the glass. This attraction causes the water to be pulled toward the glass. The water on the paper that is placed in the partially filled glass is pulled toward the edge, carrying the lightweight paper circle with it. The glass that is overfilled with water does not have the exposed glass sides for the water to be attracted to. The result is that the water molecules pull on each other with the force directed toward the center of the water's bulge. The wet paper is pulled toward the center because the water on it is pulled in this direction.

EXPERIMENT 7

POWDER DUNK

PURPOSE: To observe the wetting effect of soap and shampoo.

MATERIALS:

- liquid dish soap
- shampoo
- toothpicks
- talcum powder
- 2 soup bowls

PROCEDURE:

1. Fill both bowls with water.

2. Sprinkle a thin layer of talcum powder on the surface of the water in each bowl.

3. Dip the end of one toothpick in the shampoo, and touch the end in the center of the powder in one bowl.

4. Observe the movement of the powder.

5. Dip the end of a second toothpick in the liquid dish soap and touch the end in the center of the powder in the second bowl.

6. Observe the movement of the powder.

RESULTS Shampoo makes the talcum powder break like large floating ice blocks. The powder rushes to the sides of the bowl and starts to sink when touched by liquid dish soap.

WHY? Talcum powder is water resistant. The grains of powder float on top of the water. The water molecules on the surface are pulling equally in all directions before the shampoo or dish soap is added. The addition of the shampoo or dish soap breaks the attraction between the water molecules wherever it touches, causing the water to move outward and take the floating powder with it. The shampoo is a moderate wetting agent while the liquid dish soap is a great wetting agent. A wetting agent allows water to spread rapidly over the surface of a solid and penetrate the surface of some solids. The liquid dish soap dissolves in the water and the water quickly covers the grains of talcum powder, causing them to sink to the bottom of the bowl.

MAGIC PAPER

PURPOSE: To observe the attraction between molecules.

MATERIALS:

- 1 sheet of newspaper
- rubber cement
- scissors (These must be strong and sharp scissors, not school scissors. Ask for an adult to help with the cutting.)
- talcum powder

PROCEDURE:

1. Lay the newspaper on a table.

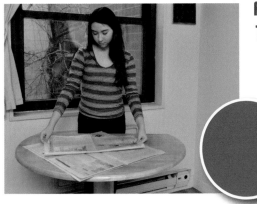

2. Evenly spread a thin but solid covering of rubber cement over one-half of the newspaper page. Note: It is important not to leave spaces uncoated or globs of glue in places.

3. Allow the rubber cement to dry for five minutes. It will feel tacky.

4. Sprinkle talcum powder evenly over the tacky cement.

5. Gently rub the powder to make sure that all of the cement is covered.

6. Cut the powdered section into 1-inch (2.54 cm) strips.

7. Hold two of the strips with the powdered sides touching.

8. Cut across the ends of the papers. Important: Do not try to snip the paper with the ends of the scissors. Insert the paper as far into the scissors as possible, cutting with the largest part of the blade.

9. Gently raise the end of one of the strips.
10. Hold only the raised edge, allowing the strip to hang.

RESULTS Instead of two separate short strips, there is one long one.

11. Hold the strips with the powdered sides together again.
12. Use the scissors to make a 45-degree diagonal cut across the ends of the paper strips.
13. Gently raise the end of one strip.
14. Hold only the raised edge, allowing the strip to hang.

RESULTS The paper strips are connected at a 45-degree angle to each other.

WHY? The powder is used to cover the cement so that the pieces do not stick together. The sharp edges of the scissors cut the paper. The pressure applied by the blades pushes a small amount of rubber cement along the cut surface. The molecules of the cement have a strong attraction for each other. These molecules are able to bridge the gap between the cut pieces and hold them together.

SPHERES OF OIL

PURPOSE: To demonstrate that gravity has little effect on bodies submerged in a liquid.

MATERIALS:

- clear drinking glass
- ½ cup (120 ml) rubbing alcohol
- ½ cup (120 ml) water
- liquid cooking oil
- eyedropper

PROCEDURE:

1. Pour ½ cup (120 ml) of water into the glass.

2. Tilt the glass and very slowly pour in ½ cup (120 ml) alcohol. Be careful not to shake the glass because the alcohol and water will mix.

3. Fill the eyedropper with the cooking oil.

4. Place the tip of the dropper below the surface of the top alcohol layer and squeeze out several drops of oil.

RESULTS The alcohol forms a layer on top of the water. The drops of oil form perfect spheres that float in the center below the alcohol and on top of the water.

WHY? Alcohol is lighter and will float on the water if the two are combined very carefully. Shaking causes them to mix, forming one solution. The oil is heavier than alcohol, but lighter than water; thus the oil drops float between the two liquids.

Gravity does not affect the drops because they are surrounded by liquid molecules that are pulling equally on them in all directions. The oil molecules pull on each other, forming a shape that takes up the least surface area, a sphere.

A HUNGRY FUNGUS

PURPOSE: To observe the production of carbon dioxide by yeast.

MATERIALS:

- soda bottle
- 2 glass quart (946 ml) jars with lids
- 1 tablespoon (13 g) lime (used in making pickles)
- 1 teaspoon sugar (4.2 g)
- ½ package powdered yeast
- 9-inch (23 cm) balloon
- 18 inches (46 cm) of aquarium tubing
- modeling clay

PROCEDURE:

1. Fill one jar with water.

2. Add 1 tablespoon (13 g) of lime and stir.

3. Secure the lid; allow the solution to stand overnight.

4. Pour off the clear liquid into the second jar. Be careful not to pour any of the lime that has settled into the bottom of the jar.

5

5. Pour ½ package of yeast into the soda bottle.
6. Fill the bottle one-half full with warm water.

7. Add 1 teaspoon (4.2 g) of sugar.

8. Place your thumb over the bottle's mouth and shake the bottle vigorously to mix the contents.

9. Place one end of the aquarium tubing in the top part of the bottle.
10. Use the clay to seal off the bottle and to hold the tubing in the bottle.

11. Insert the free end of the tube into a glass that is one-half full with the limewater you prepared earlier.

12. Observe periodically for several days.

RESULTS There is some foaming at first in the soda bottle. Bubbles of gas flow out of the tube into the limewater. The limewater turns cloudy.

WHY? Yeast is a fungus that digests sugars and starches to produce energy. In the process of producing this energy, carbon dioxide is also formed. The cloudiness of the limewater is proof that the bubbles produced by the reaction is carbon dioxide. Limewater turns cloudy only when carbon dioxide gas is bubbled through it.

HOW LONG?

PURPOSE: To time the release of bubbles produced by one Alka-Seltzer tablet.

MATERIALS:

- 1 Alka-Seltzer tablet
- soda bottle
- clay ball, the size of a walnut
- 18-inch (46 cm) piece of aquarium tubing
- jar

PROCEDURE:

1. Pour ¼ cup (60 ml) of water into the soda bottle.

2. Squeeze the clay around the tubing about 2 inches (5 cm) from one end.

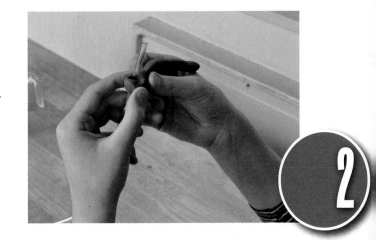

3. Fill the jar with water.

4. Place the free end of the tube in the jar of water.

5. Break the Alka-Seltzer tablet into small pieces; quickly drop the pieces into the soda bottle.

6. Immediately insert the tube into the bottle; seal the opening with the clay.

7. Record the time.

8. Watch and record the time when the bubbling stops.

RESULTS The tablet immediately reacts with the water to produce bubbles. The bubbles are released for about twenty-five minutes.

WHY? The dry acid and baking soda in the tablet are able to combine with the water to form carbon dioxide gas. It is the carbon dioxide gas that moves through the tube and forms bubbles in the glass of water. The bubbling stops when all of the material reacts.

RUST PREVENTION

PURPOSE: To observe the effect that protective coatings have on the rusting of steel wool.

MATERIALS:

- 1 steel wool soap pad
- scissors
- plate
- 1 sheet paper towel
- ½ cup (120 ml) vinegar
- pencil

1

PROCEDURE:

1. Cut the steel wool pad into four equal parts.

3

2. Run warm tap water over two of the pieces to remove as much of the soap as possible.

3. Place one piece with soap and one piece without soap in the vinegar.

4. Mark the paper towel into four equal parts. Number each section.

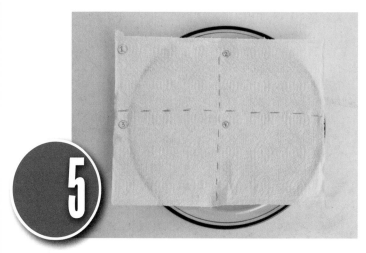

5. Lay the paper towel over a plate.

6. Remove the pieces from the vinegar and squeeze out as much liquid as possible.

7. Place the steel wool pieces in these indicated sections:

a. Section 1: Piece with no soap and soaked in vinegar.

b. Section 2: Piece with soap and soaked in vinegar.

c. Section 3: Piece with no soap, but wet with water.

d. Section 4: Dry piece with soap. This is the control.

8. Observe the steel wool pieces every ten minutes for one hour and then allow them to stand for twenty-four hours.

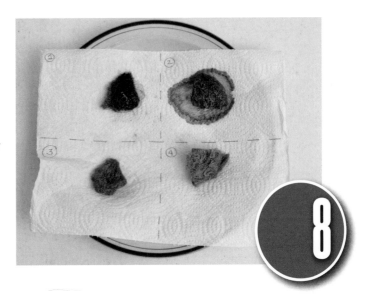

RESULTS The piece with no soap that has been soaked in vinegar shows signs of rusting after ten minutes. It takes up to one hour for the piece with soap that was soaked in vinegar to rust. After twenty-four hours, the vinegar-soaked pieces have equally rusted and the piece wet with water and containing no soap shows only slight rusting. No change is seen in the control. Note: A control is any material that is not changed at the start of the experiment.

WHY? Steel wool contains iron, which rusts by combining with oxygen in the air. Soap helps to prevent air from touching the iron. The vinegar cleans off any additional coating on the steel wool, allowing the iron and oxygen to combine. The iron oxide that is formed is reddish brown in color. One usually thinks of rust as being this color, but other colors are formed when different metals rust by combining with oxygen.

13 THE GREEN BLOB

PURPOSE: To produce a green, jelly-like blob of material from mixing two liquids.

MATERIALS:

- vinegar
- steel wool
- household ammonia
- tablespoon
- 2 small baby food jars

PROCEDURE:

1. Fill one-half of one jar with steel wool.

2. Add enough vinegar to cover the steel wool.

3. Write IRON ACETATE on the side of the glass.

4. Allow the jar to stand undisturbed for five days.

5. Pour 1 tablespoon (15 ml) of the liquid iron acetate into the second jar.

6. Add 1 tablespoon (15 ml) of household ammonia and stir.

RESULTS A dark green, jelly-like substance forms immediately.

WHY? The iron in the steel wool combines with the vinegar to produce iron acetate. Household ammonia's chemical name is ammonium hydroxide. A chemical reaction occurs as soon as these two liquids combine. The word equation for the reaction is:

ammonium hydroxide + iron acetate yields
ammonium acetate + iron hydroxide

Notice that there is an exchange of materials. Nothing new was produced. There is still ammonium, iron, hydroxide, and acetate, but the recombination produces a totally different result. The original materials were liquids and the product is a gel. The starting materials in a chemical reaction break apart and are rearranged to form the products. There are never new basic materials produced.

DRINKABLE IRON

PURPOSE: To test for the presence of iron in fruit juices.

MATERIALS:

- 1-pint (473 ml) glass jar
- 3 tea bags
- pineapple juice
- apple juice
- white grape juice
- cranberry juice
- 5 clear plastic glasses
- tablespoon

PROCEDURE:

1. Make a strong tea solution by placing the tea bags in the pint jar; then fill it with hot water.

2. Allow the jar to stand for one hour.

3. Pour 4 tablespoons (60 ml) of each juice sample into a different glass.

4. Add 4 tablespoons (60 ml) of tea to each glass and stir.

5. Allow the glasses to sit undisturbed for twenty minutes.

6. Carefully lift each glass and look up through the bottom of the glass. Make note of the juice that has dark particles settling on the bottom of the glass.

7. Allow the glasses to sit for two more hours.

8. Again, look for dark particles on the bottom of the glasses.

RESULTS Dark brown particles may be seen in some of the juices after only twenty minutes. The particles may be seen in all of the juices after two hours.

WHY? A chemical change takes place that is evident by the solid particles that form. The particles are solid and the juices are liquids, which is an indication that something new has been produced. Iron in the juices combines with chemicals in the tea to form the dark particles. The quantity of iron in the juices can vary with the brand used. Apple and pineapple generally have the most iron. Try different brands and compare their results. If the amount of iron is very small, no particles will be visible.

GROWING ICE

PURPOSE: To demonstrate that water expands when frozen.

MATERIALS:

- 1 small baby food jar
- red or blue food coloring
- permanent marking pen
- clay, a piece the size of a marble
- straw

PROCEDURE:

1. Press the piece of clay against the inside bottom of the jar.

2. Fill the jar with water.

3. Add four or five drops of food coloring and stir.

4. Slowly lower the straw into the colored water.

5. Push the bottom end of the straw into the clay. The straw can now stand in a vertical position.

6. Slowly pour all of the water out of the jar.

7. Use the pen to mark the height of the water in the straw.

8. Place the jar in a freezer for five hours.

RESULTS The height of the frozen water is above the mark.

WHY? Water molecules are attracted to one another, and when they get close enough, they bond or stick together. They do not stack together like flat boxes, but have spaces between them. Liquid water molecules occupy less volume because at the higher temperature, the molecules are more flexible and can crowd together. As the temperature lowers, the molecules bond to form a hexagonal structure. This ice structure is not very flexible and takes up more space than the same number of liquid water molecules.

TRY THIS Allow the jar to stand at room temperature until the ice in the straw melts.

RESULTS The height of the liquid water is again at the mark on the straw.

CHILLING EFFECT

PURPOSE: To cool off a thermometer.

MATERIALS:

- outdoor thermometer
- cotton ball
- rubbing alcohol

PROCEDURE:

1. Lay the thermometer on a table undisturbed for three minutes; this will allow it to register the room's temperature.

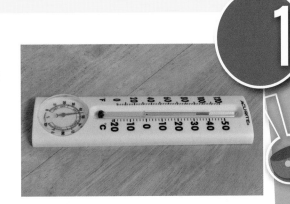

2. Blow your breath across the thermometer bulb about fifteen times.

RESULTS The liquid in the thermometer rises.

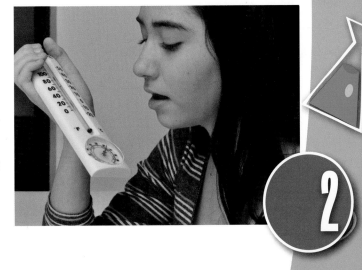

3. Moisten a cotton ball about the size of a walnut with rubbing alcohol.

4. Spread a thin layer of the wet cotton across the bulb of the thermometer.

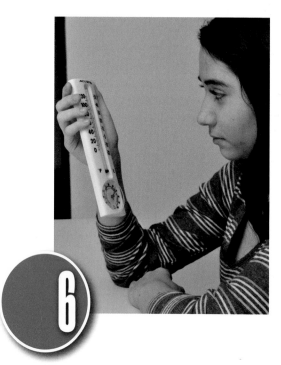

5. Blow your breath across the wet cotton about fifteen times.

6. Observe change to the temperature.

RESULTS The liquid in the thermometer moved downward.

WHY? The temperature of one's breath is about 98.6°F (37°C), which is higher than the air temperature in the room. The heat from your breath warmed the liquid in the thermometer and caused it to expand. "Expand" means that the molecules move farther apart and take up more space, thus the rise of the liquid in the thermometer.

The cooling effect of the alcohol is due to the evaporation of the alcohol around the thermometer bulb. Evaporation occurs when a liquid absorbs enough heat energy to change from a liquid to a gas. The alcohol takes energy away from the liquid in the thermometer bulb when it evaporates, causing the liquid to cool. Liquids contract when cooled. "Contract" means the molecules get closer together and take up less space, thus the liquid in the thermometer moves down.

NEEDLES

PURPOSE: To determine why planets move smoothly around the sun.

MATERIALS:

- saucer
- 1 sheet of dark construction paper
- Epsom salt
- 1 small baby food jar with a lid
- tablespoon
- scissors

PROCEDURE:

1. Fill the jar one-half full with water.

2. Add 2 tablespoons (40 g) of Epsom salt to the water.

3. Secure the lid.

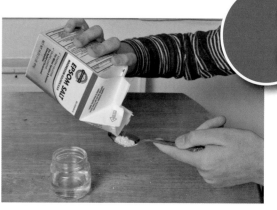

4. Shake the jar vigorously sixty times, then allow it to stand.

5. Cut a circle from the construction paper to fit the inside of the saucer.

6. Pour a thin layer of the salt solution over the paper. Try not to pour out the undissolved salt.

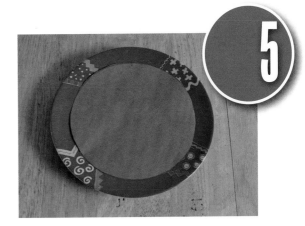

7. Place the saucer in a warm place and wait several days.

RESULTS Long, slender, needle-shaped crystals form on the paper.

WHY? Epsom salt crystals are long and slender. The particles in the box have been crushed for packaging and do not have a slender shape. As the water evaporates from the solution, small, unseen crystals start to stack together. Further evaporation increases the building process, and long, needle-shaped crystals are produced.

TYNDALL EFFECT

PURPOSE: To observe that suspensions are cloudy and contain solid floating parts that can be seen.

MATERIALS:

- scissors
- cardboard box
- 2 clear drinking glasses
- 1 teaspoon (7 g) flour
- flashlight

PROCEDURE:

1. Turn the cardboard box upside down.
2. Use the point of a pencil to make a small hole in the end of the box. The height of the hole should be one-half the height of the glass being used.

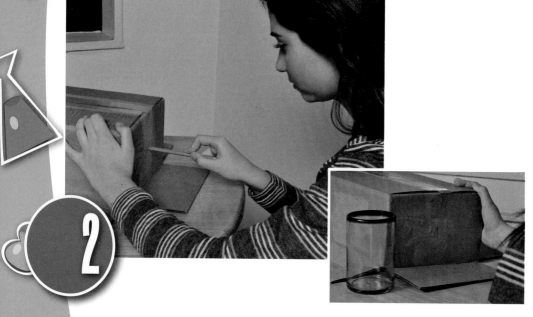

3. Cut a 1-inch (2.54 cm) square viewing hole in one side of the box. The hole must be about 3 inches (7.62 cm) from the corner of the box and as high as the small round hole on the side.

4. Fill the glasses three-quarters full with water.

5. Add 1 teaspoon (7 g) of flour to one of the glasses with water and stir.

6. Place the glass containing water and flour under the box. Position the glass so that it is in front of the viewing hole.

7. Hold the flashlight near the small hole.

8. Observe the effect that the liquid has on the light rays.

9. Put the glass containing only water under the box.

10. Shine the light through the hole and observe the effect that water has on the light rays.

RESULTS The mixture of flour and water looked cloudy. Tiny particles of flour could be seen floating in the water. The glass of water had no effect on the light rays. They passed through the water unchanged.

WHY? Flour and water form a suspension. A suspension has tiny particles floating in the liquid. The particles stay suspended until gravity pulls them down. The suspended particles stop some of the light rays. Light hits the bits of flour floating in the water and is reflected. "Reflect" means to bounce back. There is nothing in the water to reflect the light. Reflection of light by suspended particles is called the Tyndall effect, named after the British scientist John Tyndall.

PUFF SIGNALS

PURPOSE: To observe the movement of hot colored water through cooler clear water.

MATERIALS:

- 2 large-mouthed, clear, glass quart (946 ml) jars
- red food coloring
- small baby food jar
- 6-inch (15.5 cm) square of aluminum foil
- rubber band
- pencil
- 4 or 5 ice cubes

PROCEDURE:

1. Place the ice cubes in one of the quart jars. Fill the jar with cold water.

2. Fill the baby food jar to over-flowing with hot tap water. Add and stir in six or seven drops of food coloring.

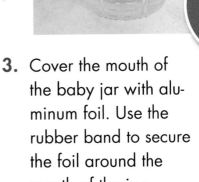

3. Cover the mouth of the baby jar with aluminum foil. Use the rubber band to secure the foil around the mouth of the jar.

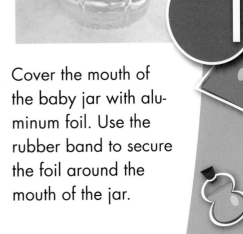

4. Stand the baby food jar inside the empty wide-mouthed jar.

5. Remove any unmelted ice cubes from the other jar and pour the chilled water into the container with the baby food jar. Completely fill the jar with the cold water.

6. Use the point of the pencil to make a small hole in the aluminum foil.

7. Slowly and gently tap the foil with the eraser of the pencil.

RESULTS The hot colored water puffs upward like smoke rings.

WHY? Water molecules, like all matter, are spaced closer together when cold and farther apart when heated. The colored hot water weighs less than the colder clear water because of this spacing. The lighter hot water rises to the top of the heavier chilled water.

TRY THIS: Punch a second hole into the foil.

RESULTS A stream of colored water starts and continues to flow out of the jar.

WHY? The cold water sinks into one of the holes, pushing the lighter hot water out.

ACID-BASE TESTING

PURPOSE: To use cabbage paper to test for the presence of an acid or base.

MATERIALS:

- coffee filters
- strainer
- 2 quart jars with lids
- 1 quart (950 ml) distilled water
- uncooked purple cabbage
- cookie sheet
- quart bowl
- scissors
- Ziploc bag
- 1 sheet of notebook paper
- 2 eyedroppers
- vinegar
- household ammonia
- 2 small baby food jars

PROCEDURE:

1. Fill one quart jar with cabbage leaves.

2. Have an adult help you heat the distilled water to boiling.

3. Fill the jar containing the leaves with the water.

4. Allow the jar to cool to room temperature.

5. Pour the cooled cabbage solution through the strainer into the second quart jar. Discard the cabbage leaves.

6. Pour one cup of cabbage juice into the bowl.
7. Dip one piece of filter paper into the cabbage juice.
8. Place the wet paper on the cookie sheet and continue until it is filled with papers.
9. Allow the papers to dry.
10. Cut the papers into strips about 1x3 inches (2.54 x 7.62 cm). (Store extras in a Ziploc bag for later.)
11. Fill one of the small jars one-quarter full with vinegar and place an eyedropper in it.
12. Fill the second jar one-quarter full with ammonia and place an eyedropper in the jar.
13. Place the notebook paper on the cookie sheet.
14. Lay the piece of cabbage testing paper on top of the notebook paper.

15. On one end of the cabbage paper place two drops of vinegar.

16. Add two drops of ammonia to the opposite end of the cabbage paper.

RESULTS Ammonia turns the paper green, and vinegar produces a pink color.

WHY? Cabbage testing paper is used to test for the presence of acids or bases. The chemicals in the cabbage juice always produce the same color changes. Bases change the paper to green, and acids produce a pink-to-red color. The cabbage paper in this lab indicates that ammonia is a basic chemical and that vinegar is acidic.

21 STRONG-STRONGER

PURPOSE: To observe the color effect that different acid concentrations have on the cabbage testing solution.

MATERIALS:

- cabbage indicator (that you made in the Acid-Base Testing experiment)
- scissors
- filter paper
- cookie sheet
- teaspoon
- alum
- cream of tartar
- Fruit Fresh (a fruit protector used in canning and freezing)

PROCEDURE:

1. Place ½ teaspoon (8 g) of alum, cream of tartar, and Fruit Fresh on the cookie sheet about 3 inches (7.62 cm) apart.

1

2. Dip the end of one of the filter strips in the cabbage solution. Lay the wet end over the mound of alum.

3. Wet a second filter strip with cabbage juice and lay over the cream of tartar.

4. The third filter strip is to be wet with the cabbage juice and placed over the Fruit Fresh.

5. Wait five minutes.

RESULTS Alum turns the cabbage paper purple, cream of tartar turns the paper pink, and the Fruit Fresh produces a rose color.

WHY? The amount of acid present determines the final color change. A strong acid will produce a red color. This test indicates that Fruit Fresh has the highest concentration of acid, cream of tartar is next in concentration, and the alum has the least amount of acid. The purple color is produced by the combination of the blue in the test solution and the small amount of red caused by the acid properties in the alum.

BAKING WITH ACID?

PURPOSE: To observe the effect that an acid has on baking.

MATERIALS:

- vinegar
- 6 cups
- 2 teaspoons
- 2 tablespoons
- baking powder
- baking soda
- 2 sheets of paper

PROCEDURE:

1. Fill one cup one-half full with vinegar.
2. Fill another cup with water.
3. Separate the two sheets of paper and lay them on a table.

3

69

4. Place two cups on each sheet of paper.

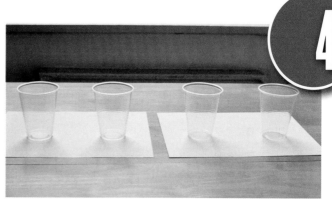

5. Put 1 teaspoon (4 g) of baking powder in two of the cups sitting on one of the sheets of paper. Write BAKING POWDER on the paper, and #1 in front of one cup and #2 in front of the other cup.

6. Use a clean teaspoon to place 1 teaspoon (4 g) of baking soda in the remaining two cups. Write BAKING SODA on the paper. Number the cups #3 and #4.

7. Start with the baking power cups. Add 2 tablespoons (30 ml) of water to cup # 1. Add 2 tablespoons (30 ml) of vinegar to cup #2.

8. Observe the results. It is always best to write down observations. Use the paper the cups are sitting on to record the results.
9. Add 2 tablespoons (30 ml) of water to cup #3, which contains baking soda.
10. Add 2 tablespoons (30 ml) of vinegar to cup #4, which also contains baking soda.
11. Observe and record the results.

RESULTS Foam is produced in cups #1, #2, and #4 when the liquid is added. Cup #3 makes only a thick milky-looking solution.

WHY? Baking powder is a mixture of sodium bicarbonate, acid, and other materials. Water activates the powdered acid. The activated acid reacts with the sodium bicarbonate to produce carbon dioxide gas. Vinegar is an acid, and, like all acids, it reacts with sodium bicarbonate to produce carbon dioxide gas. It is the carbon dioxide gas that is needed to make a cake or bread rise during baking. The carbon dioxide pushes the batter up and heat bakes it in this elevated position. Baking soda contains sodium bicarbonate, and it will produce carbon dioxide only when combined with an acid. An acid would have to be added to a batter if baking soda was used as the source of carbon dioxide. Vinegar, cream of tartar, and buttermilk are all used as a source of acid. Any one of these substances could be used with baking soda to produce carbon dioxide gas.

GLOSSARY

acid A material that tastes sour, neutralizes bases, and turns purple cabbage juice red.

atom The smallest part of an element. It contains a positive center with negative charges spinning around the outside.

baking powder A leavening agent used in baking, containing sodium bicarbonate, one or more acid salts, and corn starch.

base A material that tastes bitter, neutralizes acids, and turns purple cabbage juice green.

concentration The amount of a component in a given area or volume.

contract To become smaller by drawing closer together.

distilled Removing impurities by boiling the substance and then condensing the steam into a clean container.

evaporation The changing of a liquid to a gas by increasing the heat content of the liquid.

expand To spread out; to get larger.

gravity The force that pulls objects on the earth toward the center of the earth.

laboratory A facility that provides controlled conditions in which research and experiments may be performed.

matter The substance things are made of. Matter takes up space and has inertia and mass.

molecules The linking of two or more atoms produces a molecule.

particles Small fragments of something.

starch A large molecule found in living cells. It combines with iodine to form a distinctive blue-black color.

suspension A mixture of two materials; one does not dissolve in the other but temporarily stays suspended in the liquid until gravity pulls it down.

Tyndall effect Reflection of light by particles suspended in a solvent.

vacuum A space empty of matter.

volume Space occupied by matter.

yeast A member of the fungus family that is unicellular and reproduces by budding.

American Association for the Advancement of Science (AAAS)
1200 New York Avenue NW
Washington, DC 20005
(202) 326-6400
Web site: http://www.aaas.org
The AAAS is an international nonprofit organization dedicated to advancing science around the world by serving
   as an educator, leader, spokesperson, and professional
   association.

American Chemical Society (ACS)
1155 16th Street NW
Washington, DC 20036
(800) 227-5558
Web site: http://www.acs.org
The ACS is the world's largest scientific society that represents professionals in all fields of chemistry and sciences
   that involve chemistry. It is committed to "improving peo-
   ple's lives through the transforming power of chemistry."

American Chemistry Council (ACC)
1300 Wilson Boulevard
Arlington, VA 22209
(703) 741-5000
Web site: http://www.americanchemistry.com
The ACC represents manufacturers working to protect the envi-
   ronment, public health, and security of the United States.

American Institute of Chemists (AIC)
315 Chestnut Street
Philadelphia, PA 19106
(215) 873-8224
Web site: http://www.theaic.org
The AIC is a group of professional chemists and chemical
    engineers that offers professional certification and award
    programs for scientists, including Nobel Prize winners,
    who have advanced their fields.

Chemical Heritage Foundation (CHF)
315 Chestnut Street
Philadelphia, PA 19106
(215) 925-2222
Web site: http://www.chemheritage.org
The CHF is dedicated to preserving and promoting the his-
    tory of chemistry.

Web Sites

Due to the changing nature of Internet links, Rosen Publishing
has developed an online list of Web sites related to the subject
of this book. This site is updated regularly. Please use this link to
access the list:

http://www.rosenlinks.com/scif/chem

FOR FURTHER READING

Aloian, Molly. *Mixtures and Solutions*. New York, NY: Crabtree, 2008.

Belval, Brian. *The Carbon Elements: Carbon, Silicon, Germanium, Tin, Lead*. New York, NY: Rosen, 2009.

Brent, Lynnette. *Acids and Bases*. New York, NY: Crabtree, 2008.

Brown, Cynthia Light. *Amazing Kitchen Chemistry Projects You Can Build Yourself*. White River Junction, VT: Nomad Press, 2008.

Dingle, Adrian, and Simon Basher. *Basher Science: The Periodic Table: Elements with Style!* New York, NY: Kingfisher Books, 2010.

Field, Jon Eben. *Cleaning Chemistry*. New York, NY: Crabtree, 2011.

Field, Jon Eben. *Kitchen Chemistry*. New York, NY: Crabtree, 2011.

Field, Jon Eben. *Medicine Cabinet Chemistry*. New York, NY: Crabtree, 2011.

Frith, Alex, and Lisa Jane Gillespie. *What's Chemistry All About?* London, England: Usborne Pub, 2010.

Gardner, Robert. *Ace Your Science Project Using Chemistry Magic and Toys: Great Science Fair Ideas*. Berkeley Heights, NJ: Enslow, 2009.

Gardner, Robert. *Chemistry Science Fair Projects Using Inorganic Stuff*. Berkeley Heights, NJ: Enslow, 2010.

Gardner, Robert, Salvatore Tocci, and Kenneth G. Rainis. *Ace Your Chemistry Science Project: Great Science Fair Ideas*. Berkeley Heights, NJ: Enslow, 2009.

Heos, Bridget. *The Alkaline Earth Metals: Beryllium, Magnesium, Calcium, Strontium, Barium, Radium.* New York, NY: Rosen, 2009.

Knight, Erin. *Chemistry Around the House.* New York, NY: Crabtree, 2011.

Newmark, Ann. *Chemistry.* New York, NY: DK Eyewitness, 2005.

Rhratigan, Joe, and Veronika Gunter. *Cool Chemistry Concoctions: 50 Formulas That Fizz, Foam, Splatter & Ooze.* Asheville, NC: Lark Books, 2007.

Roza, Greg. *The Halogen Elements: Flourine, Chlorine, Bromine, Iodine, Astatine.* New York, NY: Rosen, 2010.

INDEX

About The Author

Janice VanCleave is a former school science teacher and a captivating presenter at museums, schools, and bookstores nationwide. She is the author of more than twenty other science books for children.

Photo Credits

All photos by Cindy Reiman, assisted by Karen Huang.

Designer: Nicole Russo; Editor: Bethany Bryan